50 Flavors of the Far East Recipes

By: Kelly Johnson

Table of Contents

- Pad Thai
- Sushi Rolls with Salmon and Avocado
- Sweet and Sour Chicken
- Teriyaki Beef Skewers
- Thai Green Curry with Shrimp
- Korean BBQ Beef Bulgogi
- Dim Sum (Steamed Dumplings)
- Vietnamese Pho
- Thai Mango Sticky Rice
- Chinese Hot and Sour Soup
- Japanese Ramen
- Beef Rendang
- Chinese Egg Drop Soup
- Tom Yum Soup
- Korean Kimchi Stew
- Japanese Miso Soup
- Japanese Tempura
- Thai Red Curry Chicken
- Chinese Orange Chicken
- Szechuan Stir-Fry
- Banh Mi Sandwich
- Thai Basil Chicken
- Japanese Tonkatsu
- Chinese Sweet and Sour Pork
- Vietnamese Summer Rolls
- Japanese Yakitori
- Cantonese Char Siu Pork
- Thai Pineapple Fried Rice
- Vietnamese Grilled Pork Chops
- Korean Kimchi Pancakes
- Chinese Chow Mein
- Thai Pad Kee Mao
- Japanese Gyoza (Dumplings)
- Sichuan Mapo Tofu
- Chinese Peking Duck

- Thai Green Papaya Salad
- Japanese Sushi Bowls
- Korean Spicy Pork Belly
- Chinese Scallion Pancakes
- Malaysian Laksa
- Indonesian Nasi Goreng
- Thai Lemongrass Chicken
- Chinese Salt and Pepper Shrimp
- Japanese Katsu Curry
- Chinese Kung Pao Chicken
- Vietnamese Pho Ga (Chicken Pho)
- Thai Red Curry Beef
- Korean Banchan (Side Dishes)
- Japanese Shabu Shabu
- Indonesian Satay Skewers

Pad Thai

Ingredients:

- 8 oz rice noodles
- 1 tablespoon vegetable oil
- 1/2 lb shrimp or chicken, sliced
- 2 eggs, beaten
- 1/4 cup peanuts, crushed
- 1/4 cup green onions, chopped
- 1/4 cup bean sprouts
- 2 tablespoons soy sauce
- 2 tablespoons fish sauce
- 1 tablespoon sugar
- 1 tablespoon lime juice
- 1/2 teaspoon chili flakes (optional)
- Fresh cilantro for garnish

Instructions:

1. Cook the rice noodles according to package instructions and set aside.
2. In a large skillet, heat vegetable oil over medium heat. Add shrimp or chicken and cook until browned, about 3-4 minutes.
3. Push the protein to one side and pour beaten eggs into the pan. Scramble until cooked through.
4. Add the cooked noodles, soy sauce, fish sauce, sugar, and lime juice. Toss to combine.
5. Garnish with peanuts, green onions, bean sprouts, cilantro, and chili flakes. Serve immediately.

Sushi Rolls with Salmon and Avocado

Ingredients:

- 2 cups sushi rice, cooked and seasoned
- 4 sheets nori (seaweed)
- 1/2 lb fresh sushi-grade salmon, sliced into strips
- 1 avocado, sliced
- 1 cucumber, julienned
- Soy sauce for dipping
- Wasabi (optional)
- Pickled ginger (optional)

Instructions:

1. Lay a sheet of nori on a bamboo sushi mat, shiny side down.
2. Wet your hands and spread a thin layer of rice over the nori, leaving about an inch at the top.
3. Place a few strips of salmon, avocado, and cucumber in a line across the center of the rice.
4. Roll the sushi tightly using the bamboo mat, sealing the edge with a little water.
5. Slice the roll into bite-sized pieces and serve with soy sauce, wasabi, and pickled ginger.

Sweet and Sour Chicken

Ingredients:

- 1 lb chicken breast, cut into bite-sized pieces
- 1/2 cup cornstarch
- 1 egg, beaten
- 2 tablespoons vegetable oil
- 1/2 cup bell peppers, chopped
- 1/4 cup onion, chopped
- 1/2 cup pineapple chunks
- 1/4 cup sugar
- 1/4 cup vinegar
- 1/4 cup ketchup
- 2 tablespoons soy sauce
- 1 tablespoon cornstarch mixed with 2 tablespoons water

Instructions:

1. Coat the chicken pieces in cornstarch, then dip them in the beaten egg.
2. Heat oil in a large pan over medium-high heat. Fry the chicken pieces until golden and crispy, about 4-5 minutes. Set aside.
3. In the same pan, cook the bell peppers, onion, and pineapple for 2-3 minutes.
4. Stir in the sugar, vinegar, ketchup, soy sauce, and cornstarch mixture. Cook until the sauce thickens.
5. Add the fried chicken to the sauce and toss to coat. Serve with rice.

Teriyaki Beef Skewers

Ingredients:

- 1 lb beef sirloin or flank steak, cut into bite-sized cubes
- 1/4 cup soy sauce
- 2 tablespoons honey
- 1 tablespoon rice vinegar
- 1 tablespoon sesame oil
- 2 cloves garlic, minced
- 1 tablespoon grated ginger
- 1 tablespoon sesame seeds (optional)
- Green onions for garnish

Instructions:

1. In a bowl, whisk together soy sauce, honey, rice vinegar, sesame oil, garlic, and ginger to make the marinade.
2. Place the beef cubes in the marinade and let sit for at least 30 minutes, or up to overnight.
3. Preheat the grill or grill pan to medium-high heat. Thread the beef onto skewers.
4. Grill the skewers for 2-3 minutes on each side until browned and cooked to your desired level of doneness.
5. Sprinkle with sesame seeds and garnish with green onions. Serve immediately.

Thai Green Curry with Shrimp

Ingredients:

- 1 lb shrimp, peeled and deveined
- 1 tablespoon vegetable oil
- 1 onion, chopped
- 1 can (14 oz) coconut milk
- 2 tablespoons green curry paste
- 1 tablespoon fish sauce
- 1 tablespoon sugar
- 1/2 cup chicken broth
- 1/4 cup fresh basil leaves
- 1 tablespoon lime juice
- Rice for serving

Instructions:

1. Heat oil in a pan over medium heat. Add onion and cook until softened, about 3-4 minutes.
2. Stir in the green curry paste and cook for 1 minute.
3. Pour in the coconut milk, chicken broth, fish sauce, and sugar. Bring to a simmer and cook for 5 minutes.
4. Add the shrimp and cook until pink and cooked through, about 3-4 minutes.
5. Stir in lime juice and basil leaves. Serve with rice.

Korean BBQ Beef Bulgogi

Ingredients:

- 1 lb beef (ribeye or sirloin), thinly sliced
- 3 tablespoons soy sauce
- 2 tablespoons sesame oil
- 1 tablespoon sugar
- 2 tablespoons rice vinegar
- 2 tablespoons garlic, minced
- 1 tablespoon ginger, minced
- 1/4 cup green onions, chopped
- 1 tablespoon sesame seeds
- Lettuce leaves for wrapping (optional)

Instructions:

1. In a bowl, combine soy sauce, sesame oil, sugar, rice vinegar, garlic, and ginger.
2. Add the sliced beef to the marinade and let sit for at least 30 minutes, or up to overnight.
3. Heat a grill or skillet over medium-high heat. Cook the marinated beef in batches for 2-3 minutes per side until browned and cooked through.
4. Sprinkle with sesame seeds and green onions. Serve with lettuce leaves for wrapping, if desired.

Dim Sum (Steamed Dumplings)

Ingredients:

- 1/2 lb ground pork or chicken
- 1/4 cup chopped green onions
- 1 tablespoon soy sauce
- 1 tablespoon oyster sauce
- 1 tablespoon sesame oil
- 1 teaspoon grated ginger
- 1/4 cup finely chopped cabbage
- 1 package dumpling wrappers (round)
- Soy sauce for dipping

Instructions:

1. In a bowl, combine ground pork, green onions, soy sauce, oyster sauce, sesame oil, ginger, and cabbage.
2. Place a teaspoon of filling in the center of each dumpling wrapper.
3. Fold the wrapper over the filling to create a half-moon shape, pinching the edges to seal.
4. Steam the dumplings in a bamboo or metal steamer for 8-10 minutes until cooked through.
5. Serve with soy sauce for dipping.

Vietnamese Pho

Ingredients:

- 1 lb beef (flank steak or brisket), thinly sliced
- 1 onion, halved
- 1 piece of ginger (3-inch), sliced
- 2 star anise
- 1 cinnamon stick
- 1 tablespoon coriander seeds
- 6 cups beef broth
- 2 tablespoons fish sauce
- 1 tablespoon sugar
- 1 package rice noodles
- Fresh herbs (basil, cilantro, mint)
- Bean sprouts
- Lime wedges
- Jalapeño slices
- Hoisin sauce and sriracha (optional)

Instructions:

1. In a dry pan, toast the onion, ginger, star anise, cinnamon stick, and coriander seeds over medium heat for 2-3 minutes until fragrant.
2. Add the toasted spices to a large pot with beef broth, fish sauce, and sugar. Simmer for 30 minutes.
3. Cook the rice noodles according to package instructions and divide among serving bowls.
4. Strain the broth and pour over the noodles.
5. Top with sliced beef, fresh herbs, bean sprouts, lime wedges, and jalapeño. Serve with hoisin sauce and sriracha if desired.

Thai Mango Sticky Rice

Ingredients:

- 1 cup sticky rice (glutinous rice)
- 1 1/4 cup coconut milk
- 1/4 cup sugar
- 1/4 teaspoon salt
- 2 ripe mangoes, peeled and sliced
- Sesame seeds or mung beans for garnish (optional)

Instructions:

1. Rinse the sticky rice under cold water until the water runs clear. Soak the rice in water for at least 1 hour.
2. Steam the soaked rice for 20-30 minutes, or until tender.
3. In a saucepan, combine coconut milk, sugar, and salt. Heat over medium heat until the sugar dissolves, then remove from heat.
4. Once the rice is cooked, pour the coconut milk mixture over the rice and stir to combine. Let it sit for about 10 minutes to allow the flavors to absorb.
5. Serve the sticky rice with sliced mangoes on top, garnished with sesame seeds or mung beans.

Chinese Hot and Sour Soup

Ingredients:

- 4 cups chicken broth
- 1/2 cup shiitake mushrooms, sliced
- 1/2 cup bamboo shoots, sliced
- 1/4 cup tofu, sliced into strips
- 2 tablespoons soy sauce
- 1 tablespoon rice vinegar
- 1 tablespoon sugar
- 1 teaspoon chili paste (or to taste)
- 1 tablespoon cornstarch mixed with 2 tablespoons water
- 1 egg, beaten
- 1/4 cup green onions, chopped
- 1 teaspoon sesame oil

Instructions:

1. In a large pot, bring the chicken broth to a simmer.
2. Add the mushrooms, bamboo shoots, and tofu to the broth. Let it simmer for 5-7 minutes.
3. Stir in the soy sauce, rice vinegar, sugar, and chili paste. Taste and adjust the seasoning if needed.
4. Slowly pour in the cornstarch mixture while stirring until the soup thickens slightly.
5. Drizzle in the beaten egg in a thin stream while stirring gently to create egg ribbons.
6. Remove from heat and stir in the green onions and sesame oil before serving.

Japanese Ramen

Ingredients:

- 4 cups chicken or pork broth
- 2 cups water
- 2 tablespoons soy sauce
- 1 tablespoon miso paste
- 1 tablespoon sesame oil
- 2 packs of ramen noodles
- 2 soft-boiled eggs
- 1/2 cup sliced green onions
- 1/2 cup cooked pork belly or chicken
- 1/2 cup bamboo shoots (optional)
- Nori (seaweed), sliced (optional)
- Chili oil (optional)

Instructions:

1. In a pot, combine the chicken broth, water, soy sauce, miso paste, and sesame oil. Bring it to a simmer.
2. Cook the ramen noodles according to the package instructions, then drain.
3. Divide the noodles into bowls. Pour the broth mixture over the noodles.
4. Top with sliced green onions, pork belly or chicken, soft-boiled eggs, bamboo shoots, and nori.
5. Drizzle with chili oil if desired, and serve hot.

Beef Rendang

Ingredients:

- 1 lb beef (chuck or brisket), cut into cubes
- 2 tablespoons vegetable oil
- 1 onion, chopped
- 4 cloves garlic, minced
- 1 tablespoon ginger, minced
- 1 tablespoon turmeric powder
- 1 teaspoon ground cumin
- 1 teaspoon ground coriander
- 1 can (14 oz) coconut milk
- 1/2 cup beef broth
- 2 tablespoons soy sauce
- 1 tablespoon brown sugar
- 2-3 dried red chilies (optional)
- Salt to taste
- Fresh cilantro for garnish

Instructions:

1. Heat oil in a large pot over medium heat. Add the onion, garlic, and ginger, and sauté until fragrant.
2. Add the beef cubes and brown on all sides.
3. Stir in turmeric, cumin, and coriander, and cook for 1 minute.
4. Add coconut milk, beef broth, soy sauce, sugar, and dried chilies. Bring to a simmer.
5. Cover and cook on low for 2-3 hours, or until the beef is tender and the sauce has thickened.
6. Season with salt and garnish with fresh cilantro before serving.

Chinese Egg Drop Soup

Ingredients:

- 4 cups chicken broth
- 1 tablespoon soy sauce
- 1/2 teaspoon grated ginger
- 2 eggs, beaten
- 1 tablespoon cornstarch mixed with 2 tablespoons water
- 1/4 cup green onions, chopped
- Salt and pepper to taste

Instructions:

1. In a pot, bring chicken broth to a boil. Add soy sauce and ginger.
2. Slowly stir in the cornstarch mixture to thicken the broth.
3. Reduce the heat to low. Slowly drizzle the beaten eggs into the broth while stirring gently to create egg ribbons.
4. Add chopped green onions and season with salt and pepper.
5. Serve hot.

Tom Yum Soup

Ingredients:

- 4 cups chicken or vegetable broth
- 2 stalks lemongrass, cut into pieces and smashed
- 3-4 kaffir lime leaves
- 3-4 slices galangal or ginger
- 1-2 Thai bird's eye chilies, smashed (optional)
- 1/2 lb shrimp, peeled and deveined
- 1 cup mushrooms, sliced
- 2 tablespoons fish sauce
- 1 tablespoon lime juice
- 1 teaspoon sugar
- Fresh cilantro for garnish

Instructions:

1. Bring the broth to a boil. Add lemongrass, lime leaves, galangal (or ginger), and chilies. Let it simmer for 5-7 minutes.
2. Add the shrimp and mushrooms. Cook until the shrimp turns pink and the mushrooms are tender.
3. Stir in fish sauce, lime juice, and sugar. Taste and adjust the seasoning if necessary.
4. Garnish with fresh cilantro and serve hot.

Korean Kimchi Stew (Kimchi Jjigae)

Ingredients:

- 2 cups kimchi, chopped
- 1/2 lb pork belly or beef, sliced
- 1 onion, chopped
- 1 tablespoon gochugaru (Korean red chili flakes)
- 1 tablespoon soy sauce
- 1 tablespoon sesame oil
- 4 cups beef or vegetable broth
- 1/2 block tofu, sliced
- 2 green onions, chopped
- 1 tablespoon miso paste (optional)

Instructions:

1. Heat sesame oil in a pot over medium heat. Add the pork belly or beef and cook until browned.
2. Add the onion and cook until softened. Stir in gochugaru and soy sauce.
3. Add the kimchi and broth. Bring to a simmer and cook for 10-15 minutes.
4. Add tofu and cook for another 5 minutes.
5. Stir in miso paste if using, and season with salt or soy sauce to taste.
6. Garnish with green onions and serve hot.

Japanese Miso Soup

Ingredients:

- 4 cups dashi (Japanese stock)
- 2 tablespoons miso paste (white or red)
- 1/2 block tofu, cubed
- 2 tablespoons green onions, chopped
- 1 sheet nori (seaweed), cut into strips (optional)

Instructions:

1. Bring the dashi to a simmer in a pot.
2. In a small bowl, dissolve miso paste with a small amount of warm dashi, then stir it into the pot.
3. Add tofu cubes and cook for 2-3 minutes until heated through.
4. Stir in green onions and nori if using.
5. Serve hot.

Japanese Tempura

Ingredients:

- 1 lb shrimp, peeled and deveined
- 1 small zucchini, sliced into thin rounds
- 1 small sweet potato, thinly sliced
- 1 cup all-purpose flour
- 1 egg, beaten
- 1 cup cold sparkling water
- 1 teaspoon cornstarch
- Salt, to taste
- Vegetable oil for frying

Instructions:

1. Heat oil in a deep fryer or large pot to 350°F (175°C).
2. In a bowl, whisk together flour, cornstarch, and a pinch of salt.
3. Add the egg and sparkling water, mixing until the batter is just combined (lumps are fine).
4. Dip shrimp and vegetables into the batter, coating lightly, then fry in batches for 2-3 minutes, until golden and crispy.
5. Remove from oil and drain on paper towels. Serve with dipping sauce (soy sauce, rice vinegar, and a little sugar).

Thai Red Curry Chicken

Ingredients:

- 1 lb chicken breast, sliced into strips
- 1 tablespoon vegetable oil
- 1 onion, chopped
- 1 bell pepper, sliced
- 2 tablespoons Thai red curry paste
- 1 can (14 oz) coconut milk
- 1 tablespoon fish sauce
- 1 tablespoon brown sugar
- 1 tablespoon lime juice
- Fresh basil for garnish
- Cooked rice for serving

Instructions:

1. Heat oil in a large skillet over medium heat. Add onion and bell pepper, cooking for 3-4 minutes until soft.
2. Add chicken and cook until browned.
3. Stir in the red curry paste and cook for 1 minute, then pour in the coconut milk.
4. Add fish sauce, brown sugar, and lime juice, and simmer for 10-12 minutes until the sauce thickens and the chicken is cooked through.
5. Serve over cooked rice and garnish with fresh basil.

Chinese Orange Chicken

Ingredients:

- 1 lb chicken breast, cut into bite-sized pieces
- 1/2 cup all-purpose flour
- 2 tablespoons cornstarch
- 1 egg, beaten
- 1/2 cup orange juice
- 1/4 cup soy sauce
- 1 tablespoon rice vinegar
- 1 tablespoon sugar
- 1 teaspoon grated ginger
- 1 clove garlic, minced
- 1 tablespoon cornstarch mixed with 2 tablespoons water
- 2 tablespoons vegetable oil for frying
- Orange zest for garnish

Instructions:

1. Mix flour, cornstarch, and a pinch of salt in a bowl. Dip chicken pieces into the beaten egg, then dredge in the flour mixture.
2. Heat oil in a pan over medium-high heat. Fry chicken in batches until golden and crispy, then set aside on paper towels.
3. In a saucepan, combine orange juice, soy sauce, rice vinegar, sugar, ginger, and garlic. Bring to a simmer and cook for 5 minutes.
4. Stir in cornstarch-water mixture and cook until the sauce thickens.
5. Toss the fried chicken in the orange sauce until well coated. Garnish with orange zest and serve.

Szechuan Stir-Fry

Ingredients:

- 1 lb chicken or beef, thinly sliced
- 1 tablespoon vegetable oil
- 1 red bell pepper, sliced
- 1 zucchini, sliced
- 1 onion, sliced
- 2 tablespoons soy sauce
- 1 tablespoon rice vinegar
- 2 tablespoons Szechuan peppercorns
- 1 tablespoon chili paste
- 2 cloves garlic, minced
- 1 tablespoon cornstarch mixed with 2 tablespoons water
- Cooked rice for serving

Instructions:

1. Heat oil in a large skillet or wok over medium-high heat. Add the chicken or beef and stir-fry until browned, about 5 minutes.
2. Add the vegetables and stir-fry for another 3-4 minutes.
3. Stir in soy sauce, rice vinegar, Szechuan peppercorns, chili paste, and garlic, and cook for another 1-2 minutes.
4. Mix in the cornstarch mixture and cook until the sauce thickens.
5. Serve the stir-fry over rice.

Banh Mi Sandwich

Ingredients:

- 1 baguette or 4 small baguette rolls
- 1/2 lb pork, grilled or roasted, thinly sliced
- 1 cucumber, thinly sliced
- 1/4 cup cilantro leaves
- 1/4 cup pickled carrots and daikon radish (or just pickled carrots)
- 1 jalapeno, sliced
- 1 tablespoon mayonnaise
- 1 tablespoon soy sauce

Instructions:

1. Slice the baguette lengthwise, leaving it hinged.
2. Spread mayonnaise on the inside of the bread.
3. Layer the pork, cucumber, cilantro, pickled vegetables, and jalapeno.
4. Drizzle with soy sauce and close the sandwich.
5. Serve immediately.

Thai Basil Chicken

Ingredients:

- 1 lb ground chicken
- 1 tablespoon vegetable oil
- 2 cloves garlic, minced
- 2 Thai bird's eye chilies, minced (or 1 red chili)
- 1 tablespoon soy sauce
- 1 tablespoon fish sauce
- 1 teaspoon sugar
- 1/2 cup fresh basil leaves, chopped
- Cooked rice for serving

Instructions:

1. Heat oil in a pan over medium heat. Add garlic and chilies, and stir-fry for 1-2 minutes until fragrant.
2. Add ground chicken and cook until browned.
3. Stir in soy sauce, fish sauce, and sugar, and cook for 2-3 minutes.
4. Add the chopped basil leaves and cook until wilted.
5. Serve with rice.

Japanese Tonkatsu

Ingredients:

- 4 pork cutlets (tonkatsu)
- 1/2 cup flour
- 2 eggs, beaten
- 1 cup panko breadcrumbs
- 1/2 cup vegetable oil for frying
- Tonkatsu sauce (store-bought or homemade)

Instructions:

1. Season the pork cutlets with salt and pepper. Dredge each cutlet in flour, dip into the beaten eggs, and coat with panko breadcrumbs.
2. Heat oil in a deep pan over medium heat. Fry the pork cutlets for 4-5 minutes per side, until golden and crispy.
3. Drain the cutlets on paper towels. Slice the tonkatsu and drizzle with tonkatsu sauce before serving.

Chinese Sweet and Sour Pork

Ingredients:

- 1 lb pork tenderloin, cut into bite-sized cubes
- 1/2 cup cornstarch
- 1 egg, beaten
- 2 tablespoons vegetable oil
- 1 bell pepper, sliced
- 1 onion, sliced
- 1/2 cup pineapple chunks
- 1/4 cup rice vinegar
- 1/4 cup sugar
- 1/4 cup ketchup
- 2 tablespoons soy sauce
- 1/4 cup water

Instructions:

1. Toss pork cubes in cornstarch and dip them in the beaten egg.
2. Heat oil in a pan over medium-high heat. Fry the pork until golden and crispy, then set aside on paper towels.
3. In the same pan, stir-fry bell pepper, onion, and pineapple for 2-3 minutes.
4. In a bowl, whisk together rice vinegar, sugar, ketchup, soy sauce, and water. Pour into the pan with the vegetables and simmer for 3-4 minutes.
5. Add the fried pork back into the pan, tossing to coat with the sauce.
6. Serve hot.

Vietnamese Summer Rolls

Ingredients:

- 8 rice paper wrappers
- 1/2 lb shrimp, peeled and deveined, cooked
- 1/2 cucumber, julienned
- 1/2 carrot, julienned
- 1/2 cup fresh mint leaves
- 1/2 cup fresh cilantro leaves
- 1/2 cup fresh basil leaves
- 1/2 cup vermicelli noodles, cooked
- 1 tablespoon hoisin sauce (for dipping)
- 1 tablespoon peanut butter (for dipping)
- 1 tablespoon lime juice (for dipping)

Instructions:

1. Fill a shallow dish with warm water. Dip each rice paper wrapper into the water for 5-10 seconds, until softened.
2. Lay the softened wrapper on a flat surface and arrange shrimp, cucumber, carrot, herbs, and noodles in the center.
3. Fold the sides of the rice paper in and roll tightly.
4. Repeat with the remaining ingredients.
5. Mix hoisin sauce, peanut butter, and lime juice to make a dipping sauce. Serve with summer rolls.

Japanese Yakitori

Ingredients:

- 1 lb chicken thighs, boneless and skinless, cut into bite-sized pieces
- 1/2 onion, sliced
- 1/4 cup soy sauce
- 2 tablespoons mirin
- 2 tablespoons sake
- 1 tablespoon sugar
- 1 teaspoon sesame oil
- Skewers (soaked in water if wooden)

Instructions:

1. In a bowl, whisk together soy sauce, mirin, sake, sugar, and sesame oil to make the marinade.
2. Add chicken pieces and onion slices to the marinade. Refrigerate for 30 minutes.
3. Thread chicken and onion alternately onto skewers.
4. Preheat a grill or grill pan over medium heat. Grill the skewers for 5-6 minutes on each side, basting with the marinade.
5. Serve hot.

Cantonese Char Siu Pork

Ingredients:

- 1 lb pork shoulder or pork belly, cut into strips
- 2 tablespoons hoisin sauce
- 2 tablespoons soy sauce
- 1 tablespoon rice wine
- 1 tablespoon honey
- 1 teaspoon Chinese five-spice powder
- 1 clove garlic, minced
- 1/4 teaspoon red food coloring (optional)

Instructions:

1. In a bowl, mix hoisin sauce, soy sauce, rice wine, honey, Chinese five-spice powder, garlic, and food coloring (if using).
2. Coat the pork strips with the marinade and refrigerate for at least 4 hours or overnight.
3. Preheat the oven to 400°F (200°C). Line a baking sheet with aluminum foil and place a rack on top.
4. Roast the pork for 25-30 minutes, brushing with additional marinade halfway through.
5. Serve sliced with rice.

Thai Pineapple Fried Rice

Ingredients:

- 2 cups cooked jasmine rice, chilled
- 1/2 cup pineapple, chopped into small pieces
- 1/4 cup peas and carrots, frozen or fresh
- 2 eggs, scrambled
- 1/4 cup cashews, roasted
- 1 tablespoon soy sauce
- 1 tablespoon fish sauce
- 1 teaspoon curry powder
- 1 tablespoon vegetable oil
- 2 cloves garlic, minced
- Fresh cilantro and lime wedges for garnish

Instructions:

1. Heat oil in a large skillet or wok over medium heat. Add garlic and cook until fragrant.
2. Add peas and carrots, cooking until tender. Add the scrambled eggs and stir until cooked through.
3. Stir in the rice, pineapple, cashews, soy sauce, fish sauce, and curry powder. Cook, stirring frequently, for 5-6 minutes.
4. Garnish with fresh cilantro and lime wedges. Serve hot.

Vietnamese Grilled Pork Chops

Ingredients:

- 4 bone-in pork chops
- 2 tablespoons fish sauce
- 1 tablespoon soy sauce
- 2 tablespoons sugar
- 1 clove garlic, minced
- 1 tablespoon lemongrass, minced
- 1 tablespoon vegetable oil
- 1/2 teaspoon ground black pepper
- Fresh cilantro for garnish

Instructions:

1. In a bowl, mix fish sauce, soy sauce, sugar, garlic, lemongrass, vegetable oil, and black pepper to make the marinade.
2. Place the pork chops in the marinade, ensuring they are coated well. Marinate for at least 1 hour.
3. Preheat the grill to medium-high heat. Grill the pork chops for 5-6 minutes on each side, until fully cooked.
4. Garnish with fresh cilantro and serve.

Korean Kimchi Pancakes

Ingredients:

- 1 cup kimchi, chopped
- 1/2 cup all-purpose flour
- 1/4 cup rice flour
- 1/2 cup water
- 1 egg
- 2 tablespoons sesame oil
- 2 tablespoons vegetable oil
- 1/2 teaspoon gochugaru (Korean chili flakes)
- Soy sauce for dipping

Instructions:

1. In a bowl, mix kimchi, all-purpose flour, rice flour, water, egg, sesame oil, and gochugaru to make a batter.
2. Heat vegetable oil in a pan over medium heat. Pour in batter to form small pancakes, cooking for 2-3 minutes on each side until crispy and golden.
3. Serve with soy sauce for dipping.

Chinese Chow Mein

Ingredients:

- 8 oz chow mein noodles, cooked
- 1 tablespoon vegetable oil
- 1 onion, sliced
- 1 carrot, julienned
- 1 bell pepper, sliced
- 1/2 cup soy sauce
- 2 tablespoons oyster sauce
- 1 tablespoon hoisin sauce
- 2 cloves garlic, minced
- 2 teaspoons sesame oil
- 2 green onions, sliced

Instructions:

1. Heat vegetable oil in a large skillet or wok over medium heat. Add onions, carrots, and bell peppers, stir-frying until tender.
2. Add garlic and cook for 30 seconds, then stir in the cooked noodles.
3. In a bowl, mix soy sauce, oyster sauce, hoisin sauce, and sesame oil. Pour over the noodles and vegetables, tossing to coat.
4. Garnish with sliced green onions and serve.

Thai Pad Kee Mao (Drunken Noodles)

Ingredients:

- 8 oz wide rice noodles
- 1 tablespoon vegetable oil
- 1/2 lb chicken or beef, thinly sliced
- 1 onion, sliced
- 1 bell pepper, sliced
- 2-3 Thai bird's eye chilies, minced
- 2 cloves garlic, minced
- 1 tablespoon soy sauce
- 1 tablespoon oyster sauce
- 1 tablespoon fish sauce
- 1 teaspoon sugar
- 1/2 cup fresh Thai basil leaves

Instructions:

1. Cook the rice noodles according to package instructions. Drain and set aside.
2. Heat oil in a large skillet or wok over medium-high heat. Add the chicken or beef and cook until browned.
3. Add onion, bell pepper, chilies, and garlic, stir-frying for 2-3 minutes.
4. Stir in soy sauce, oyster sauce, fish sauce, and sugar, cooking for 1-2 minutes.
5. Add the cooked noodles and basil, tossing to combine. Cook for another 2-3 minutes.
6. Serve hot.

Japanese Gyoza (Dumplings)

Ingredients:

- 1/2 lb ground pork
- 1/4 cup cabbage, finely chopped
- 1/4 cup green onions, chopped
- 2 cloves garlic, minced
- 1 tablespoon ginger, minced
- 1 tablespoon soy sauce
- 1 tablespoon sesame oil
- 1 teaspoon salt
- 1/2 teaspoon pepper
- 20-24 gyoza wrappers
- 2 tablespoons vegetable oil (for frying)
- 1/4 cup water (for steaming)

Instructions:

1. In a bowl, combine ground pork, cabbage, green onions, garlic, ginger, soy sauce, sesame oil, salt, and pepper.
2. Place a gyoza wrapper in the palm of your hand, add a small spoonful of the filling in the center. Moisten the edges with water, fold the wrapper in half, and pleat the edges to seal.
3. Heat vegetable oil in a pan over medium heat. Place gyoza in the pan and cook for 2-3 minutes until the bottoms are golden.
4. Add water to the pan and cover, steaming the dumplings for 4-5 minutes until the water evaporates.
5. Serve hot with dipping sauce.

Sichuan Mapo Tofu

Ingredients:

- 1 lb tofu, cubed
- 1/2 lb ground pork (optional)
- 2 tablespoons vegetable oil
- 2 tablespoons Sichuan peppercorns
- 2 cloves garlic, minced
- 2 tablespoons ginger, minced
- 2 tablespoons doubanjiang (fermented chili paste)
- 1 tablespoon soy sauce
- 1 tablespoon rice wine
- 1/4 cup chicken broth
- 1 teaspoon cornstarch, mixed with 2 teaspoons water
- 1/4 cup green onions, chopped
- Rice for serving

Instructions:

1. Heat vegetable oil in a pan over medium heat. Add Sichuan peppercorns, garlic, and ginger, and sauté until fragrant.
2. Add ground pork (if using) and cook until browned.
3. Stir in doubanjiang, soy sauce, rice wine, and chicken broth. Bring to a simmer.
4. Gently add tofu cubes to the pan and cook for 3-4 minutes.
5. Add cornstarch mixture to thicken the sauce. Stir in green onions.
6. Serve hot with rice.

Chinese Peking Duck

Ingredients:

- 1 whole duck (about 5-6 lbs)
- 1 tablespoon Chinese five-spice powder
- 2 tablespoons soy sauce
- 1 tablespoon honey
- 1 tablespoon rice vinegar
- 1/4 cup hoisin sauce
- 8-10 thin pancakes (or Chinese steamed buns)
- Cucumber and green onion for garnish

Instructions:

1. Preheat the oven to 375°F (190°C).
2. Rub the duck with Chinese five-spice powder and season with soy sauce.
3. Mix honey and rice vinegar, brush this mixture onto the duck.
4. Roast the duck for 1.5 to 2 hours, basting every 30 minutes with the honey-vinegar mixture.
5. Once crispy, remove the duck and allow it to rest before slicing.
6. Serve the duck with hoisin sauce, pancakes, cucumber, and green onions.

Thai Green Papaya Salad

Ingredients:

- 1 small green papaya, peeled and shredded
- 1/4 cup cherry tomatoes, halved
- 1/4 cup green beans, cut into 1-inch pieces
- 2 cloves garlic, minced
- 1-2 Thai bird's eye chilies, minced
- 1 tablespoon fish sauce
- 1 tablespoon lime juice
- 1 tablespoon sugar
- 1/4 cup roasted peanuts, crushed
- 1/4 cup dried shrimp (optional)

Instructions:

1. In a mortar and pestle, crush garlic and chilies.
2. Add fish sauce, lime juice, and sugar to the mortar and mix well.
3. In a large bowl, combine shredded papaya, tomatoes, and green beans.
4. Pour the dressing over the vegetables and toss to combine.
5. Garnish with crushed peanuts and dried shrimp (if using). Serve immediately.

Japanese Sushi Bowls

Ingredients:

- 1 cup sushi rice, cooked
- 1/2 lb sashimi-grade salmon, cubed
- 1/2 cucumber, thinly sliced
- 1/4 avocado, sliced
- 1 tablespoon soy sauce
- 1 teaspoon rice vinegar
- 1 teaspoon sesame oil
- 1/4 cup edamame (optional)
- 1 tablespoon sesame seeds
- Nori strips for garnish

Instructions:

1. Cook sushi rice according to package instructions. Allow it to cool.
2. In a bowl, combine soy sauce, rice vinegar, and sesame oil. Toss the salmon cubes in this marinade.
3. Assemble bowls by placing rice at the bottom. Top with marinated salmon, cucumber, avocado, and edamame.
4. Sprinkle sesame seeds and nori strips over the top. Serve chilled or at room temperature.

Korean Spicy Pork Belly

Ingredients:

- 1 lb pork belly, thinly sliced
- 2 tablespoons gochujang (Korean chili paste)
- 1 tablespoon soy sauce
- 1 tablespoon sesame oil
- 2 cloves garlic, minced
- 1 tablespoon brown sugar
- 1/2 teaspoon ground black pepper
- 2 tablespoons vegetable oil
- 1/2 onion, sliced
- 2 green onions, chopped
- Rice for serving

Instructions:

1. In a bowl, mix gochujang, soy sauce, sesame oil, garlic, brown sugar, and black pepper.
2. Toss the pork belly slices in the marinade and refrigerate for 30 minutes.
3. Heat vegetable oil in a pan over medium-high heat. Add the pork belly and cook until browned and crispy, about 8-10 minutes.
4. Add onions and cook for another 2 minutes.
5. Serve hot with rice and garnish with green onions.

Chinese Scallion Pancakes

Ingredients:

- 2 cups all-purpose flour
- 3/4 cup boiling water
- 1/2 teaspoon salt
- 1/4 cup sesame oil
- 4 green onions, chopped
- Vegetable oil for frying

Instructions:

1. In a bowl, combine flour and salt. Gradually add boiling water, stirring with chopsticks or a fork to form a dough.
2. Knead the dough for 5-7 minutes until smooth. Cover and let rest for 30 minutes.
3. Divide dough into 4 portions. Roll each portion into a thin circle.
4. Brush with sesame oil and sprinkle with chopped green onions. Roll the dough into a cylinder and then coil it into a round shape.
5. Roll the coiled dough out again into a pancake. Heat vegetable oil in a skillet and fry the pancakes for 2-3 minutes on each side until crispy.
6. Serve hot with dipping sauce.

Malaysian Laksa

Ingredients:

- 200g rice noodles
- 1 tablespoon vegetable oil
- 200g cooked shrimp or chicken
- 1/2 cup coconut milk
- 1 tablespoon red curry paste
- 1 tablespoon tamarind paste
- 2 cups chicken broth
- 2 boiled eggs, halved
- 1/2 cucumber, julienned
- 2 tablespoons cilantro, chopped
- 1 tablespoon lime juice

Instructions:

1. Cook the rice noodles according to package instructions, then drain and set aside.
2. Heat vegetable oil in a large pot. Add curry paste and cook until fragrant.
3. Add coconut milk, tamarind paste, and chicken broth. Bring to a simmer and cook for 5 minutes.
4. Add the shrimp or chicken to the broth and cook for another 3 minutes.
5. Divide noodles into bowls and ladle the soup over them. Top with boiled eggs, cucumber, cilantro, and lime juice.
6. Serve hot.

Indonesian Nasi Goreng

Ingredients:

- 2 cups cooked jasmine rice (preferably day-old)
- 2 tablespoons vegetable oil
- 2 cloves garlic, minced
- 1 small onion, diced
- 1/2 cup cooked chicken or shrimp, diced
- 1/4 cup frozen peas
- 2 eggs, beaten
- 2 tablespoons soy sauce
- 1 tablespoon sweet soy sauce (kecap manis)
- 1 teaspoon sambal oelek (or chili paste)
- 1/2 cucumber, sliced (for garnish)
- Fried shallots (optional, for garnish)
- Fresh cilantro (optional, for garnish)

Instructions:

1. Heat oil in a large pan or wok over medium heat. Add garlic and onion and sauté until fragrant.
2. Add the cooked chicken or shrimp and peas, and stir-fry for 2-3 minutes.
3. Push the mixture to one side of the pan. Add the beaten eggs to the other side and scramble until cooked.
4. Add the rice to the pan, breaking up any clumps. Stir in soy sauce, sweet soy sauce, and sambal oelek.
5. Cook for 3-4 minutes, stirring constantly, until everything is well combined.
6. Serve garnished with cucumber slices, fried shallots, and cilantro.

Thai Lemongrass Chicken

Ingredients:

- 1 lb chicken thighs, boneless and skinless, sliced
- 2 stalks lemongrass, chopped and minced
- 3 cloves garlic, minced
- 1 tablespoon fish sauce
- 1 tablespoon soy sauce
- 1 tablespoon brown sugar
- 1 tablespoon lime juice
- 1 teaspoon ground turmeric
- 2 tablespoons vegetable oil
- 1/4 cup fresh cilantro, chopped
- 1/2 teaspoon chili flakes (optional)

Instructions:

1. In a bowl, combine lemongrass, garlic, fish sauce, soy sauce, brown sugar, lime juice, and turmeric. Add the chicken and marinate for 30 minutes.
2. Heat oil in a large skillet or wok over medium-high heat. Add the marinated chicken and cook for 5-7 minutes until golden brown and cooked through.
3. Garnish with fresh cilantro and chili flakes, if using. Serve with rice.

Chinese Salt and Pepper Shrimp

Ingredients:

- 1 lb large shrimp, peeled and deveined
- 2 tablespoons cornstarch
- 1/2 teaspoon salt
- 1/2 teaspoon black pepper
- 1/4 teaspoon white pepper (optional)
- 2 tablespoons vegetable oil
- 2 cloves garlic, minced
- 1-2 Thai bird's eye chilies, chopped
- 1/4 cup green onions, chopped

Instructions:

1. In a bowl, toss the shrimp with cornstarch, salt, black pepper, and white pepper.
2. Heat oil in a pan or wok over high heat. Add the shrimp and cook for 2-3 minutes on each side until golden and crispy.
3. Remove the shrimp and set aside. In the same pan, add garlic, chilies, and green onions. Stir-fry for 1-2 minutes until fragrant.
4. Return the shrimp to the pan and toss everything together. Serve immediately.

Japanese Katsu Curry

Ingredients:

- 2 boneless pork chops
- 1/4 cup flour
- 1 egg, beaten
- 1/2 cup panko breadcrumbs
- 2 tablespoons vegetable oil
- 1 onion, sliced
- 2 carrots, chopped
- 2 potatoes, diced
- 2 tablespoons curry powder
- 1 tablespoon soy sauce
- 2 cups chicken broth
- 1 tablespoon honey
- Rice for serving

Instructions:

1. Bread the pork chops by dredging them in flour, then dipping in egg, and coating with panko breadcrumbs.
2. Heat vegetable oil in a pan over medium heat. Fry the pork chops for 4-5 minutes per side until golden brown and cooked through. Set aside.
3. In the same pan, sauté onions, carrots, and potatoes for 5-7 minutes. Add curry powder, soy sauce, chicken broth, and honey. Bring to a simmer and cook for 10-15 minutes until the vegetables are tender.
4. Slice the katsu (pork chop) and serve over rice, topped with the curry sauce.

Chinese Kung Pao Chicken

Ingredients:

- 1 lb chicken breast, diced
- 2 tablespoons soy sauce
- 1 tablespoon rice wine
- 1 tablespoon cornstarch
- 1 tablespoon vegetable oil
- 1/4 cup dried red chilies
- 1/4 cup unsalted roasted peanuts
- 2 cloves garlic, minced
- 1 tablespoon ginger, minced
- 1 tablespoon soy sauce
- 1 tablespoon hoisin sauce
- 1 tablespoon sugar
- 1/4 cup chicken broth

Instructions:

1. In a bowl, mix chicken, soy sauce, rice wine, and cornstarch. Set aside for 10 minutes.
2. Heat oil in a pan over medium heat. Add dried chilies and cook for 1 minute.
3. Add garlic and ginger and cook for another 30 seconds.
4. Add chicken to the pan and cook until browned. Add soy sauce, hoisin sauce, sugar, and chicken broth. Stir to combine and cook for 2-3 minutes.
5. Stir in peanuts and cook for 1 more minute. Serve hot with rice.

Vietnamese Pho Ga (Chicken Pho)

Ingredients:

- 1 whole chicken (3-4 lbs)
- 1 onion, halved
- 1 piece ginger (3-inch), halved
- 3-4 star anise
- 3-4 cloves
- 1 cinnamon stick
- 1 tablespoon fish sauce
- 1 tablespoon salt
- 8 cups water
- 1 lb rice noodles
- Fresh cilantro, basil, and bean sprouts for garnish
- Lime wedges and chili slices for serving

Instructions:

1. In a large pot, add the chicken, onion, ginger, star anise, cloves, cinnamon, fish sauce, and salt. Cover with water and bring to a boil.
2. Reduce heat and simmer for 1.5 to 2 hours, skimming the surface occasionally.
3. Remove the chicken and set aside to cool. Strain the broth and discard the solids.
4. Cook rice noodles according to package instructions. Divide noodles into bowls and ladle hot broth over them.
5. Shred the chicken and add to the bowls. Garnish with cilantro, basil, bean sprouts, lime wedges, and chili slices.

Thai Red Curry Beef

Ingredients:

- 1 lb beef (such as sirloin or flank steak), thinly sliced
- 2 tablespoons vegetable oil
- 2 tablespoons red curry paste
- 1 can coconut milk (14 oz)
- 1 tablespoon fish sauce
- 1 tablespoon brown sugar
- 1/4 cup Thai basil, chopped
- 1 bell pepper, sliced
- 1/2 cup bamboo shoots (optional)
- Rice for serving

Instructions:

1. Heat oil in a large pan over medium-high heat. Add red curry paste and cook for 1-2 minutes until fragrant.
2. Add beef and stir-fry until browned, about 4-5 minutes.
3. Stir in coconut milk, fish sauce, and brown sugar. Bring to a simmer and cook for another 5-7 minutes.
4. Add bell pepper and bamboo shoots (if using). Cook for 3-4 minutes until the vegetables are tender.
5. Garnish with Thai basil and serve with rice.

Korean Banchan (Side Dishes)

Ingredients:

- 1 cup spinach, blanched
- 1/2 cup bean sprouts, blanched
- 1/4 cup kimchi
- 1/4 cup pickled radish
- 1/4 cup cucumber, thinly sliced

Instructions:

1. For spinach banchan, season the spinach with garlic, sesame oil, and salt.
2. For bean sprout banchan, season the bean sprouts with garlic, sesame oil, and salt.
3. Serve the kimchi, pickled radish, and cucumber slices as additional banchan.

Japanese Shabu Shabu

Ingredients:

- 1/2 lb thinly sliced beef (ribeye or sirloin)
- 4 cups dashi broth (or chicken broth)
- 1/2 cup soy sauce
- 1 tablespoon mirin
- 1 tablespoon sesame oil
- 1/2 cup mushrooms, sliced
- 1/2 cup napa cabbage, chopped
- 1/2 cup tofu, sliced
- Dipping sauce (ponzu, sesame)

Instructions:

1. In a large pot, combine dashi broth, soy sauce, mirin, and sesame oil. Bring to a simmer.
2. Add mushrooms, napa cabbage, and tofu to the broth and cook until tender.
3. Dip thin slices of beef into the hot broth for a few seconds, then dip into your desired dipping sauce.
4. Serve with steamed rice.

Indonesian Satay Skewers

Ingredients:

- 1 lb chicken thighs or beef, cubed
- 1 tablespoon soy sauce
- 1 tablespoon curry powder
- 1 tablespoon coconut milk
- 1 tablespoon brown sugar
- 1 clove garlic, minced
- 1 teaspoon turmeric powder
- Wooden skewers

Instructions:

1. In a bowl, mix soy sauce, curry powder, coconut milk, brown sugar, garlic, and turmeric.
2. Marinate the chicken or beef cubes in the mixture for at least 30 minutes.
3. Thread the meat onto skewers and grill on medium heat for 5-7 minutes per side.
4. Serve with peanut sauce and rice.

www.ingramcontent.com/pod-product-compliance
Lightning Source LLC
LaVergne TN
LVHW081337060526
838201LV00055B/2701